Girls on the Run

A Running Themed Journal

Activinotes

DAILY JOURNALS, PLANNERS, NOTEBOOKS AND OTHER BLANK BOOKS

Day   Route :   Date

_____

Time : _____

Distance : _____

Pace : _____

Notes :

Running Buddies : _____

Day   Route :   Date

_____

Time : _____

Distance : _____

Pace : _____

Notes :

Running Buddies : _____

Day   Route :   Date

_____

Time : _____

Distance : _____

Pace : _____

Notes :

Running Buddies : _____

Day   Route :   Date

_____

Time : _____

Distance : _____

Pace : _____

Notes :

Running Buddies : _____

Day   Route :   Date

_____

Time : _____

Distance : _____

Pace : _____

Notes :

Running Buddies : _____

Day   Route :   Date

_____

Time : _____

Distance : _____

Pace : _____

Notes :

Running Buddies : _____

Day   Route :   Date

_____

Time : _____

Distance : _____

Pace : _____

Notes :

Running Buddies : _____

Day　　　　　　　　Route :　　　　　　　　Date

_____

Time : _____

Distance : _____

Pace : _____

Notes :

Running Buddies : _____

Day   Route :   Date

_____

Time : _____

Distance : _____

Pace : _____

Notes :

Running Buddies : _____

Day   Route :   Date

_____

Time : _____

Distance : _____

Pace : _____

Notes :

Running Buddies : _____

Day   Route :   Date

_____

Time : _____

Distance : _____

Pace : _____

Notes :

Running Buddies : _____

Day   Route :   Date

_____

Time : _____

Distance : _____

Pace : _____

Notes :

Running Buddies : _____

Day   Route :   Date

_____

Time : _____

Distance : _____

Pace : _____

Notes :

Running Buddies : _____

Day   Route :   Date

_____

Time : _____

Distance : _____

Pace : _____

Notes :

Running Buddies : _____

Day   Route :   Date

_____

Time : _____

Distance : _____

Pace : _____

Notes :

Running Buddies : _____

Day   Route :   Date

_____

Time : _____

Distance : _____

Pace : _____

Notes :

Running Buddies : _____

Day   Route :   Date

_____

Time : _____

Distance : _____

Pace : _____

Notes :

Running Buddies : _____

Day   Route :   Date

_____

Time : _____

Distance : _____

Pace : _____

Notes :

Running Buddies : _____

Day   Route :   Date

_____

Time : _____

Distance : _____

Pace : _____

Notes :

Running Buddies : _____

Day   Route :   Date

_____

Time : _____

Distance : _____

Pace : _____

Notes :

Running Buddies : _____

Day   Route :   Date

_____

Time : _____

Distance : _____

Pace : _____

Notes :

Running Buddies : _____

Day   Route :   Date

_____

Time : _____

Distance : _____

Pace : _____

Notes :

Running Buddies : _____

Day

Route :

Date

_____

Time : _____

Distance : _____

Pace : _____

Notes :

Running Buddies : _____

Day   Route :   Date

_____

Time : _____

Distance : _____

Pace : _____

Notes :

Running Buddies : _____

Day   Route :   Date

_____

Time : _____

Distance : _____

Pace : _____

Notes :

Running Buddies : _____

Day   Route :   Date

_____

Time : _____

Distance : _____

Pace : _____

Notes :

Running Buddies : _____

Day   Route :   Date

_____

Time : _____

Distance : _____

Pace : _____

Notes :

Running Buddies : _____

Day   Route :   Date

_____

Time : _____

Distance : _____

Pace : _____

Notes :

Running Buddies : _____

Day   Route :   Date

_____

Time : _____

Distance : _____

Pace : _____

Notes :

Running Buddies : _____

Day   Route :   Date

_____

Time : _____

Distance : _____

Pace : _____

Notes :

Running Buddies : _____

Day   Route :   Date

_____

Time : _____

Distance : _____

Pace : _____

Notes :

Running Buddies : _____

Day   Route :   Date

_____

Time : _____

Distance : _____

Pace : _____

Notes :

Running Buddies : _____

Day   Route :   Date

_____

Time : _____

Distance : _____

Pace : _____

Notes :

Running Buddies : _____

Day   Route :   Date

_____

Time : _____

Distance : _____

Pace : _____

Notes :

Running Buddies : _____

Day   Route :   Date

_____

Time : _____

Distance : _____

Pace : _____

Notes :

Running Buddies : _____

Day   Route :   Date

_____

Time : _____

Distance : _____

Pace : _____

Notes :

Running Buddies : _____

Day   Route :   Date

_____

Time : _____

Distance : _____

Pace : _____

Notes :

Running Buddies : _____

Day

Route :

Date

_____

Time : _____

Distance : _____

Pace : _____

Notes :

Running Buddies : _____

Day   Route :   Date

_____

Time : _____

Distance : _____

Pace : _____

Notes :

Running Buddies : _____

Day   Route :   Date

_____

Time : _____

Distance : _____

Pace : _____

Notes :

Running Buddies : _____

Day   Route :   Date

_____

Time : _____

Distance : _____

Pace : _____

Notes :

Running Buddies : _____

Day   Route :   Date

_____

Time : _____

Distance : _____

Pace : _____

Notes :

Running Buddies : _____

Day   Route :   Date

_____

Time : _____

Distance : _____

Pace : _____

Notes :

Running Buddies : _____

Day   Route :   Date

_____

Time : _____

Distance : _____

Pace : _____

Notes :

Running Buddies : _____

Day   Route :   Date

_____

Time : _____

Distance : _____

Pace : _____

Notes :

Running Buddies : _____

Day   Route :   Date

_____

Time : _____

Distance : _____

Pace : _____

Notes :

Running Buddies : _____

Day   Route :   Date

_____

Time : _____

Distance : _____

Pace : _____

Notes :

Running Buddies : _____

Day   Route :   Date

_____

Time : _____

Distance : _____

Pace : _____

Notes :

Running Buddies : _____

Day   Route :   Date

_____

Time : _____

Distance : _____

Pace : _____

Notes :

Running Buddies : _____

Day   Route :   Date

_____

Time : _____

Distance : _____

Pace : _____

Notes :

Running Buddies : _____

Day   Route :   Date

_____

Time : _____

Distance : _____

Pace : _____

Notes :

Running Buddies : _____

Day   Route :   Date

_____

Time : _____

Distance : _____

Pace : _____

Notes :

Running Buddies : _____

Day

Route :

Date

_____

Time : _____

Distance : _____

Pace : _____

Notes :

Running Buddies : _____

Day   Route :   Date

_____

Time : _____

Distance : _____

Pace : _____

Notes :

Running Buddies : _____

Day   Route :   Date

_____

Time : _____

Distance : _____

Pace : _____

Notes :

Running Buddies : _____

Day   Route :   Date

_____

Time : _____

Distance : _____

Pace : _____

Notes :

Running Buddies : _____

Day   Route :   Date

_____

Time : _____

Distance : _____

Pace : _____

Notes :

Running Buddies : _____

Day   Route :   Date

_____

Time : _____

Distance : _____

Pace : _____

Notes :

Running Buddies : _____

Day   Route :   Date

_____

Time : _____

Distance : _____

Pace : _____

Notes :

Running Buddies : _____

Day   Route :   Date

_____

Time : _____

Distance : _____

Pace : _____

Notes :

Running Buddies : _____

Day   Route :   Date

_____

Time : _____

Distance : _____

Pace : _____

Notes :

Running Buddies : _____

Day

Route :

Date

_____

Time : _____

Distance : _____

Pace : _____

Notes :

Running Buddies : _____

Day   Route :   Date

_____

Time : _____

Distance : _____

Pace : _____

Notes :

Running Buddies : _____

Day   Route :   Date

_____

Time : _____

Distance : _____

Pace : _____

Notes :

Running Buddies : _____

Day   Route :   Date

_____

Time : _____

Distance : _____

Pace : _____

Notes :

Running Buddies : _____

Day   Route :   Date

_____

Time : _____

Distance : _____

Pace : _____

Notes :

Running Buddies : _____

Day   Route :   Date

_____

Time : _____

Distance : _____

Pace : _____

Notes :

Running Buddies : _____

Day   Route :   Date

_____

Time : _____

Distance : _____

Pace : _____

Notes :

Running Buddies : _____

Day   Route :   Date

_____

Time : _____

Distance : _____

Pace : _____

Notes :

Running Buddies : _____

Day   Route :   Date

_____

Time : _____

Distance : _____

Pace : _____

Notes :

Running Buddies : _____

Day   Route :   Date

_____

Time : _____

Distance : _____

Pace : _____

Notes :

Running Buddies : _____

Day   Route :   Date

_____

Time : _____

Distance : _____

Pace : _____

Notes :

Running Buddies : _____

Day   Route :   Date

_____

Time : _____

Distance : _____

Pace : _____

Notes :

Running Buddies : _____

Day   Route :   Date

_____

Time : _____

Distance : _____

Pace : _____

Notes :

Running Buddies : _____

Day   Route :   Date

_____

Time : _____

Distance : _____

Pace : _____

Notes :

Running Buddies : _____

Day

Route :

Date

_____

Time : _____

Distance : _____

Pace : _____

Notes :

Running Buddies : _____

Day   Route :   Date

_____

Time : _____

Distance : _____

Pace : _____

Notes :

Running Buddies : _____

Day   Route :   Date

_____

Time : _____

Distance : _____

Pace : _____

Notes :

Running Buddies : _____

Day   Route :   Date

_____

Time : _____

Distance : _____

Pace : _____

Notes :

Running Buddies : _____

Day   Route :   Date

_____

Time : _____

Distance : _____

Pace : _____

Notes :

Running Buddies : _____

Day   Route :   Date

_____

Time : _____

Distance : _____

Pace : _____

Notes :

Running Buddies : _____

Day   Route :   Date

_____

Time : _____

Distance : _____

Pace : _____

Notes :

Running Buddies : _____

Day   Route :   Date

_____

Time : _____

Distance : _____

Pace : _____

Notes :

Running Buddies : _____

Day   Route :   Date

_____

Time : _____

Distance : _____

Pace : _____

Notes :

Running Buddies : _____

Day   Route :   Date

_____

Time : _____

Distance : _____

Pace : _____

Notes :

Running Buddies : _____

Day   Route :   Date

_____

Time : _____

Distance : _____

Pace : _____

Notes :

Running Buddies : _____

Day   Route :   Date

_____

Time : _____

Distance : _____

Pace : _____

Notes :

Running Buddies : _____

Day   Route :   Date

_____

Time : _____

Distance : _____

Pace : _____

Notes :

Running Buddies : _____

Day   Route :   Date

_____

Time : _____

Distance : _____

Pace : _____

Notes :

Running Buddies : _____

Day   Route :   Date

_____

Time : _____

Distance : _____

Pace : _____

Notes :

Running Buddies : _____

Day   Route :   Date

_____

Time : _____

Distance : _____

Pace : _____

Notes :

Running Buddies : _____

59

Made in the USA
Lexington, KY
21 December 2018